MAY 2 1 2016

D0949013

MAY 2 1 2016

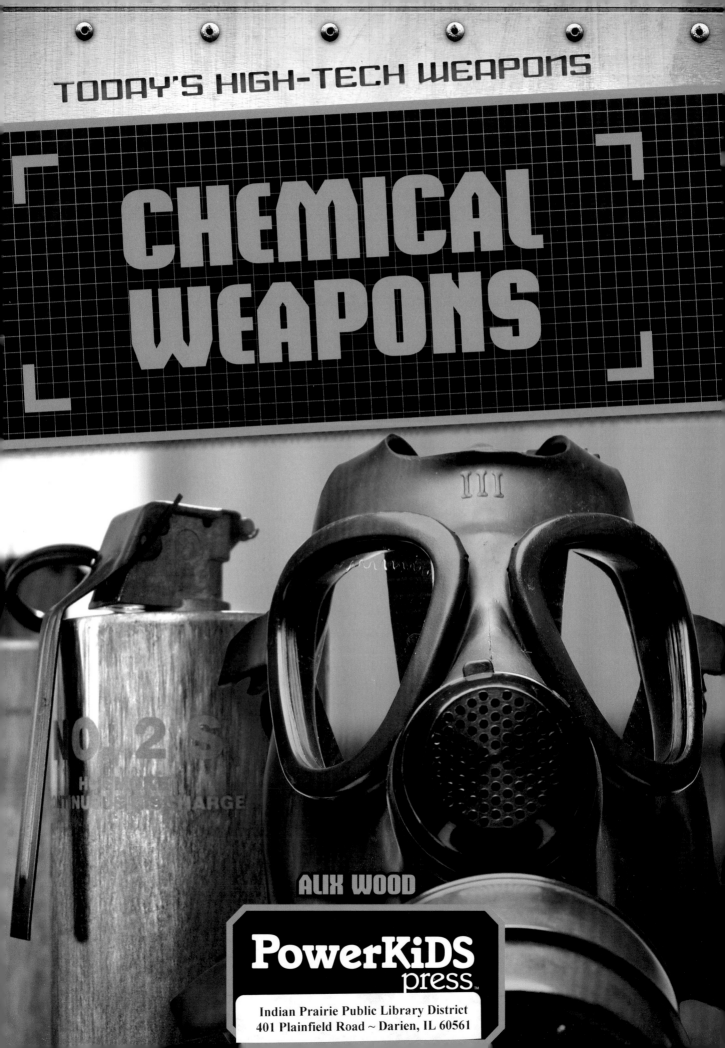

TODAY'S HIGH-TECH WEAPONS

CHEMICAL WEAPONS

ALIX WOOD

PowerKiDS press

Published in 2016 by **Rosen Publishing**
29 East 21st Street, New York, NY 10010

Cataloging-in-Publication Data

Wood, Alix.
Chemical weapons / by Alix Wood.
p. cm. — (Today's high-tech weapons)
Includes index.
ISBN 978-1-5081-4679-7 (pbk.)
ISBN 978-1-5081-4680-3 (6-pack)
ISBN 978-1-5081-4681-0 (library binding)
1. Chemical warfare — Juvenile literature. 2. Chemical weapons —
Juvenile literature. I. Wood, Alix. II. Title.
UG447.W66 2016
358'.34—d23

Editor: Eloise Macgregor
Designer: Alix Wood
Consultant: Mark Baker

Photo Credits: Cover © Shutterstock/Eky Studio (top), © Shutterstock/
optimarc (ctr), © Getty Images/Thinkstock (btm lft), © Shutterstock/
Silverscreen (btm rt); 4 © Brett Butterworth; 5, 6, 10 top © Dollar
Photo Club; 7, 23, 26 © DoD; 8 © Mohamed CJ; 9 © DoD/Pfc. Crystal
Druery; 10 bottom © DoD/Lance Cpl. Andrew Kuppers; 11 bottom
left © DoD/Lance Cpl. Scott W. Whiting; 11 bottom right © DoD/Cpl.
Demetrius Morgan; 12 © DoD/Cpl. Michael Petersheim; 13 © Imperial
War Museum; 14 © DoD/Ryan G. Wilbur; 15 top © MoD/Kate Maurer;
15 bottom © MoD/Martin Jones; 16 top © Palthrow; 17 © Dreamstime;
18 © Zerevan Chey; 19 top © DoD/Sgt. Sean Kimmons; 20 © Spetsnaz
Alpha; 25 © National Archives/Brian K. Grigsby; 27 © National
Museum of Health and Medicine; 28 © DoD/Sgt. Angelita M. Lawrence;
29 © DoD/Senior Airman Brigitte Brantley; all other images are in the
public domain

Manufactured in the United States of America
CPSIA Compliance Information: Batch #BW16PK.
For Further Information contact Rosen Publishing, New York, New York at 1-800-237-9932

CONTENTS

WHAT ARE CHEMICAL WEAPONS?

People have used **chemicals** to poison individuals throughout history. In the early days, people made the poisons from natural chemicals found in plants. During the 1900s, people began to mass-produce chemical agents and use them in warfare.

A World War I German **chlorine** gas attack at Ypres, Belgium, was one of the first such attacks. Chemical weapons caused 100,000 deaths and 1.2 million casualties during that war. At first, the Allies had no gas masks to protect against the chlorine gas.

A field ambulance doctor, Captain Francis Scrimger, realized the gas was chlorine. He told his staff to urinate on handkerchiefs and use them as a face cover. A chemical in the urine helped destroy the chlorine. Water also helped dissolve the gas in the air before soldiers breathed it in.

A gas attack during the First World War

CHEMICAL WEAPON FACT FILE:

WHO WOULD USE THE WEAPONS: Chemical weapons were mainly used by the military. Their use is now banned.

CAUSE FOR CONCERN: Once a weapon has been invented, it is impossible to "uninvent." As the knowledge to make chemical weapons is available, they could still be used.

PROTECTION AGAINST CHEMICAL WARFARE: The military and some transportation organizations have sensing devices that alert if a chemical is detected. The military have protective suits and masks to wear in the event of an attack.

Chemical weapons are now considered to be too dangerous to use. In order to control their use, and to destroy stocks of weapons, the Organization for the Prohibition of Chemical Weapons created the Chemical Weapons Convention. The convention bans chemical weapons and a country's stocks must be destroyed in an agreed time period.

The treaty has now been signed by around 189 countries. Only a small number of nations have not signed the Chemical Weapons Convention.

The international symbol for a chemical hazard

DEADLY NERVE GAS

In the early hours of August 21, 2013, several rockets hit a farming area near Damascus, Syria. The rockets contained a dangerous **nerve agent**, called **sarin**. Who fired the rockets, and why, remains a mystery, but the result was deadly. The attacks killed several hundred people and injured hundreds more.

Nerve agents disrupt how nerves transfer messages around the body. Sarin is classified as a **weapon of mass destruction** by the United Nations and has been outlawed. Most nerve agents were originally made to be used in agriculture to control insects.

Breathing a lethal dose of sarin can kill in 15 minutes. Sarin on the skin takes longer for the symptoms to occur, but can then kill in only 1-2 minutes. Livestock, pets, and wild animals were also killed in the Syrian attacks. They may have been poisoned by infected food or water, too.

SARIN FACT FILE:

TYPE: Nerve agent

APPEARANCE: Colorless, odorless gas

STRENGTH: A 0.5 milligram dose can kill a person in one minute

SPECIAL INFORMATION: Sarin is liquid at room temperature but then turns into a gas, allowing it to spread quickly

TREATMENT: The drug, atropine, can help if injected straight away. The skin and eyes must be washed thoroughly.

A person who has been exposed to a nerve agent must be treated immediately. Washing the eyes with water and the skin with water mixed with a small amount of bleach helps get rid of sarin on the skin. Drugs such as atropine can be used as an **antidote** for nerve agent poisoning. The military is usually issued with antidote kits if they are serving in an area that may be at risk of attack.

An antidote kit instruction leaflet. Soldiers must pin the used antidote to their clothing in case they fall unconscious, so medical teams know they have taken it.

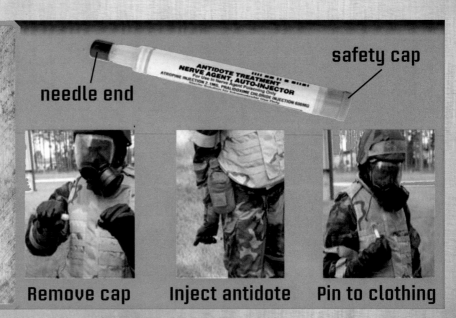

needle end

safety cap

Remove cap   Inject antidote   Pin to clothing

RIOT CONTROL

Tear gas, or CS gas, is used as a riot control agent. The gas causes people's eyes to stream with tears and it becomes impossible for them to keep their eyes open. Their nose, mouth, and throat may feel like they are burning, causing coughing and breathing difficulty. The gas would be very effective at stopping a riot.

CS gas doesn't always work, however. In 1993, the **FBI** used CS gas to try to end a long, dangerous siege at the compound of a **religious cult** in Waco, Texas. They used the gas to flush out the armed people. The plan backfired when a blaze, believed to have been started by the cult, killed 75 people.

555 CS

SPEDEHEAT GRENADE

Federal Laboratories
SALTSBURG, PENNSYLVANIA 15681

Although tear gas is described as a **nonlethal** weapon, studies have shown it can cause heart and liver damage. The use of CS in warfare is banned under the Chemical Weapons Convention, mainly because it might cause someone to use a more serious chemical weapon in response.

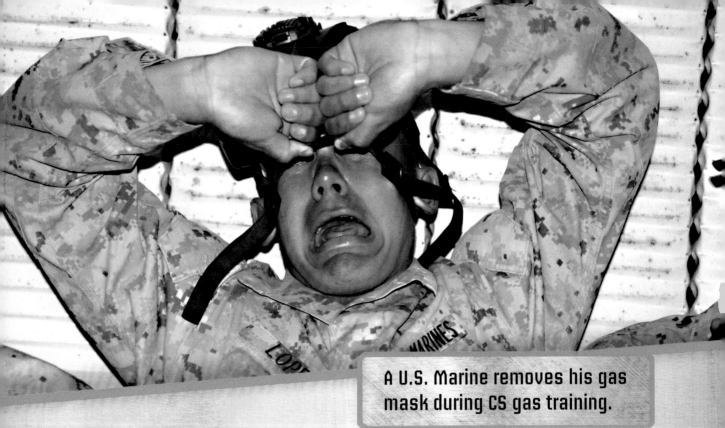

CS GAS FACT FILE:

TYPE: Riot control agent

HOW DOES IT SPREAD?: By aerosol

SYMPTOMS: Burning skin, tears streaming from eyes, nasal mucus, coughing

HOW DEADLY IS IT?: It is not deadly

TREATMENT: Washing the affected area with water. Washing any affected clothing.

In some military training, soldiers will be exposed to CS gas on purpose. Why? It helps soldiers learn to trust their protective masks. Soldiers are put in a CS gas-filled room. One by one they are asked to remove their masks and recite the alphabet, before they can leave the room. The unpleasant effects of the CS gas prove to them how well their masks were working before they took them off! The effects usually wear off after around 15 minutes.

PEPPER SPRAY

Pepper spray is made from a chemical found in chili plants. In many U.S. states, pepper spray can be bought by anyone over 18. It is used by police forces and the U.S. military as a form of riot control. The Marines are trained to use tear gas and pepper spray for self-defense, too, against people or against animals such as bears and dogs.

During training, Marines are sprayed with pepper spray. They are then attacked by various pretend enemies, who they must capture. It is a very difficult test as they can't even see through their tears!

A Marine is sprayed in the face with pepper spray as part of his nonlethal weapons training.

Pepper spray is available for purchase in many U.S. states. Just like tear gas, though, it is banned for use in war by the Chemical Weapons Convention. If troops were disabled by what appeared to be a lethal chemical weapon, they may hit back with a real one.

PEPPER SPRAY FACT FILE:

TYPE: Riot control agent

HOW DOES IT SPREAD?: By aerosol

SYMPTOMS: Tears streaming from eyes, pain, and temporary blindness which can last up to 30 minutes

HOW DEADLY IS IT?: It is not deadly

TREATMENT: Washing the affected area with water. Washing any affected clothing.

Pepper spray irritates the eyes and causes them to close. When used it may blow into the eyes of the person using it, too, so wearing a protective mask is a good idea. A high-tech pepper spray is being suggested that automatically takes a photo of the person being sprayed, with a note of the location. This information is sent to a monitoring service that can send help. This would be more useful for individuals than for a soldier, however, as their location would already be known.

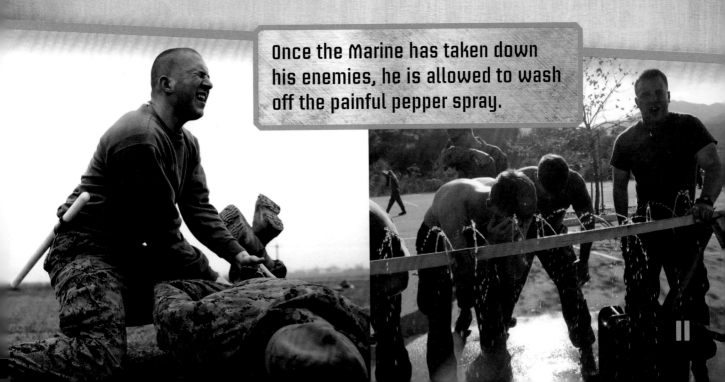

Once the Marine has taken down his enemies, he is allowed to wash off the painful pepper spray.

MUSTARD GAS

At 10:10 p.m., on July 12, 1917, near a World War I Allied trench at Ypres, Belgium, a new kind of shell fell to the ground. Quickly, the soldiers fumbled in the darkness for their rifles, helmets, and gas masks. A yellow fog spread around the trench. The fog smelled a little like mustard. Some men started spitting and sneezing, but then the smell went away, and the soldiers began to take off their masks. That may have been the worst decision they ever made.

Mustard gas lingers in the air and **contaminates** an area for some time. After an hour or more, exposure to the gas causes swelling of the eyes, vomiting, and painful skin blistering. Many Allied soldiers died from lung infections.

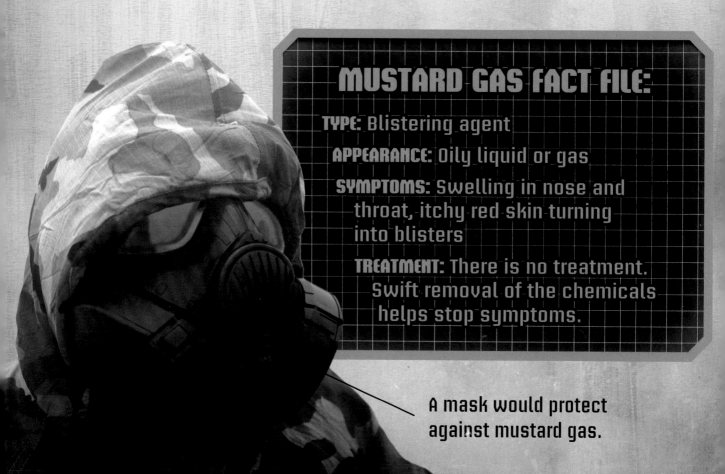

MUSTARD GAS FACT FILE:

TYPE: Blistering agent

APPEARANCE: Oily liquid or gas

SYMPTOMS: Swelling in nose and throat, itchy red skin turning into blisters

TREATMENT: There is no treatment. Swift removal of the chemicals helps stop symptoms.

A mask would protect against mustard gas.

A painting from World War I called *Gassed* by John Singer Sargent.

There is no treatment for the effects of mustard gas. The best thing to do is to avoid it by finding high ground. Mustard gas is heavier than air and will settle in low-lying areas. Soldiers are taught to take off any clothing that got sulfur mustard on it, and to wash with water. Eyes should be washed for 5 to 10 minutes. Wearing dark glasses helps sore eyes.

In recent years, fishermen working off the coasts of Denmark and Sweden have been bringing up an unwanted haul — clumps of mustard gas. After World War II, chemical weapons such as mustard agent were dumped by the Germans in the waters off Denmark and Sweden. The weapon casings have rusted over the years and allowed the liquid to leak out. In 1984, more than 30 fishing boats were contaminated, and a dozen fishermen suffered burns. In 2015, a Danish fisherman brought up an entire bomb!

CHEMICAL AGENT DETECTORS

Special detectors have been invented that can warn of chemical attacks. It is not just the military that finds these detectors useful. Industrial accidents can cause dangerous chemical releases. **Hazmat** organizations, usually part of fire departments, take care of civilian chemical leaks. Hazmat is short for hazardous materials.

The U.S. military has detectors that can sense, identify, and alert a soldier if there are any chemical warfare agents in the area. The detector is about the size of a portable CD player, and can hang on clothing, a belt, or a harness.

U.S. Navy personnel use their detector kits during an exercise.

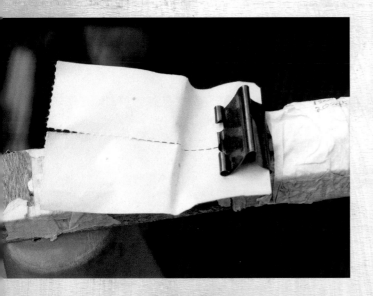

The military has some fairly low-tech methods to detect chemical weapons, too. Paper sensors like these change color within 30 seconds of exposure to even very small amounts of **toxins**.

There are more high-tech solutions. MCAD stands for Manportable Chemical Agent Detector. This piece of equipment can detect and identify chemical warfare agents and toxic industrial chemicals. A vital piece of equipment, it gives troops a few valuable extra seconds to protect themselves if they come under attack.

Nineteenth-century inventor Alexander Graham Bell discovered that gases have individual sound characteristics. Modern scientists using this knowledge have created a high-tech machine that can detect chemical threats by the sounds they make!

ZYKLON-B

When a packed train pulled into the Nazi concentration camp at Auschwitz, the prison guards waited. As each person stumbled out of the carriage into the daylight, a guard told them to go either left or right. Right meant they went to the labor camps. Left meant they were sent to the gas chambers.

The victims believed they were heading for the showers. False shower heads had been put in the gas chambers, so as not to create panic. Once the doors were shut, the guards dropped Zyklon-B pellets through holes at either end of the room and waited. They did not have to wait long.

Empty Zyklon-B canisters, found in 1945 at Auschwitz

Suitcases left by prisoners at Auschwitz

The chemical agent Zyklon-B, containing deadly cyanide poison, was used by the Nazis in the gas chambers during World War II. It was responsible for around a million deaths.

Cyanides are produced by certain bacteria, fungi, and algae. They can be found in a number of plants and their seeds and pits. Apricots, apples, and peaches have seeds and pits that contain levels of cyanide!

ZYKLON-B FACT FILE:

TYPE: Blood agent

APPEARANCE: In pellet form. The pellets turned into a lethal gas once in air.

STRENGTH: Zyklon-B could kill a person in two minutes

SPECIAL INFORMATION: Before its use in gas chambers, Zyklon-B was a common insecticide

OTHER USES: As it was an insecticide, Zyklon-B was also used at Auschwitz for killing lice on prisoners' clothes

HALABJA

On a beautiful March spring day in 1988, Iraqi MiG and Mirage aircraft dropped chemical bombs on the town of Halabja, Iraq, far from the Iraqi army base on the outskirts of the town. Clouds of white, black, and then yellow smoke rose high into the air. Birds started falling from the sky. Then people began to be affected by the gas. Survivors of the bombing said they could smell apples, then a smell similar to rotting garbage, and then the smell of eggs.

It is believed that several chemical agents were used in the attack, including mustard gas and nerve agents. Most of the wounded taken to hospitals across the border in Tehran, Iran, were suffering from mustard gas exposure.

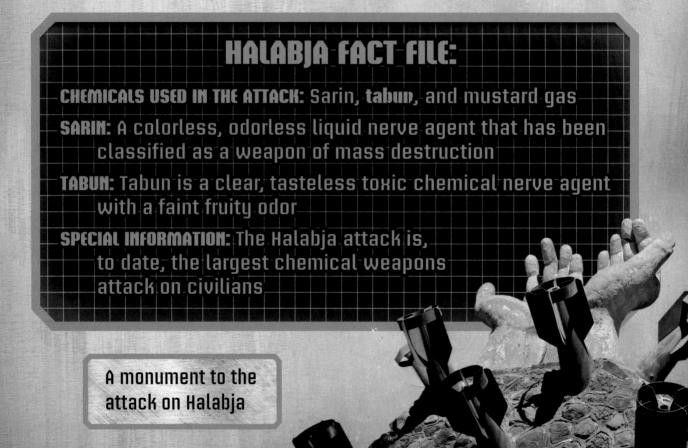

HALABJA FACT FILE:

CHEMICALS USED IN THE ATTACK: Sarin, tabun, and mustard gas

SARIN: A colorless, odorless liquid nerve agent that has been classified as a weapon of mass destruction

TABUN: Tabun is a clear, tasteless toxic chemical nerve agent with a faint fruity odor

SPECIAL INFORMATION: The Halabja attack is, to date, the largest chemical weapons attack on civilians

A monument to the attack on Halabja

A U.S. Army patrol at the cemetery at Halabja, where the victims of the chemical attack are buried

Around 12,000 people died during the attacks. Most of the victims were women and children. Years later hundreds of people are still being treated for the severe aftereffects of the attack.

Saddam Hussein's cousin Ali Hassan al-Majid was condemned to death by hanging by an Iraqi court in January 2010, after being found guilty of organizing the Halabja massacre. Hassan al-Majid was known as "Chemical Ali" for his role in gassing several villages in northern Iraq.

THE MOSCOW THEATER CRISIS

In science **fiction** movies, people are sometimes harmlessly sprayed unconscious by a fictional knockout gas. A gas that could do this does not really exist. However, during a **hostage** crisis at a Moscow theater in 2002, Russian security services pumped an undisclosed chemical agent into the building to help them raid the theater and rescue the hostages.

Armed Chechens had taken 850 hostages. After a two-and-a-half-day siege and the execution of two female hostages, special forces pumped a chemical agent into the building's ventilation system.

Russian Alpha Group special forces on a training exercise

All the Chechen attackers were killed, but unfortunately around 130 hostages died too. All except two of the hostages who died were killed by the mysterious substance pumped into the theater. The Russian authorities have refused to say what the gas was. Many hostages died because medical staff treating them did not know what the gas was, and had no idea how to treat the symptoms.

Many experts believe that the gas pumped into the theater was based on fentanyl. Fentanyl is a very strong pain relief drug. It is hundreds of times stronger than morphine, and can cause death. The symptoms can be cured, though, by using a drug known as naloxone.

MYSTERY GAS FACT FILE:

TYPE: Incapacitating agent

WHAT WAS THE GAS: The agent has never been named. It is believed to be a surgical **anesthetic** or unknown chemical weapon.

WHAT WE KNOW: Russian authorities told the U.S. Embassy what some of the effects of the gas were. From that information, doctors figured out that the gas was probably based on fentanyl. Later, the Russian Health Minister confirmed this.

ACTIQ 200

Fentanyl can be safely used in stick form for pain relief.

MAKING SAFE

As chemical weapons become more deadly, it is important to try to protect people from their use. This includes any accidental release of the chemicals. Some more modern chemical weapons are designed to be much safer. Safety is especially important to protect people who live near where the weapons are stored.

Binary chemical weapons do not contain a deadly agent. Instead, the individual substances used to make up the toxin are put in the weapon separately. The weapons can then be transported and stored more safely. The chemical reaction only takes place when the weapon is fired. Firing removes a barrier between the chemicals.

Sarin is made up of a mixture of chemicals.

M687 FACT FILE:

TYPE: Binary Chemical weapon

HOW IS IT MADE?: A chemical, known as DF, and a mixture of two other agents are placed in the weapon, separated by a partition

HOW DOES IT WORK?: When the weapon is fired, the sudden speed causes the partition to break. The chemicals mix together as the weapon spins in flight, producing sarin nerve gas.

Since chemical weapons became outlawed in 1997, countries have been hard at work destroying their stocks of weapons. Many military bases that used to produce or store the weapons have become the centers for their destruction! The chemicals are destroyed by being either **incinerated** or **neutralized**. First, the bomb casings are taken apart by robots. The chemical agent is then drained out and burned in an extremely hot furnace. The bomb casings are also placed in a metal furnace for 15 minutes.

Neutralization destroys the agent by mixing it with hot water or hot water and another chemical. The water is then sent to a hazardous waste facility for treatment and disposal. This neutralization station pictured can be carried to an area by truck. It only needs water, fuel, and a few chemicals to work!

AGENT ORANGE

Agent Orange is a **defoliant** used by the U.S. military. Defoliants are designed to kill plants. The British used defoliants to destroy crops during their conflict in Malaya. During the Vietnam War the U.S. military sprayed nearly 20 million gallons (75.7 million liters) of defoliant during Operation Ranch Hand. The goal was to kill plant life and deprive the enemy of food and cover. Unfortunately it harmed a lot more than just plants.

Agent Orange was given its name because the barrels it was shipped in had an orange stripe. Spraying was usually done from helicopters or from low-flying aircraft. By 1971, 12 percent of the total area of South Vietnam had been sprayed with the dangerous chemicals.

AGENT ORANGE FACT FILE:

TYPE: Defoliant

IS IT A WEAPON?: Agent Orange was not considered a weapon at the time, as it was meant to kill crops, not people

STRENGTH: Agent Orange was used at hundreds of times greater concentration than was considered safe by the U.S. Environmental Protection Agency

Agent Orange was believed to have been made stronger than intended by a mistake at the factory where it was made. Accidental overheating of the mixture made it into a much more deadly product. Both the people of Vietnam and any people that handled the agent suffered health issues as a result. The spraying did not just harm the enemy. It affected the ordinary people of Vietnam, too, as their crops failed and they had no food.

A helicopter spraying Agent Orange during the Vietnam conflict

Health issues caused by Agent Orange include tumors, birth defects, and cancer. The Vietnam Red Cross believes around one million Vietnamese have been affected by Agent Orange. Generations after the event, children are still born with birth defects. Many U.S. servicemen and their families were also affected.

LEWISITE

Lewisite is a blister agent that causes severe chemical burns. Painful water blisters appear on the body of those affected. It was manufactured in the U.S., Japan, and Germany for use as a chemical weapon. Lewisite contains arsenic, a deadly poison.

Several people living in China have died from accidental exposure to lewisite from stocks left by the Japanese after World War II. In 2014 the Japanese built a special facility in China to dispose of the agent.

Teams using chemical detection equipment scan for blister agents during an army exercise.

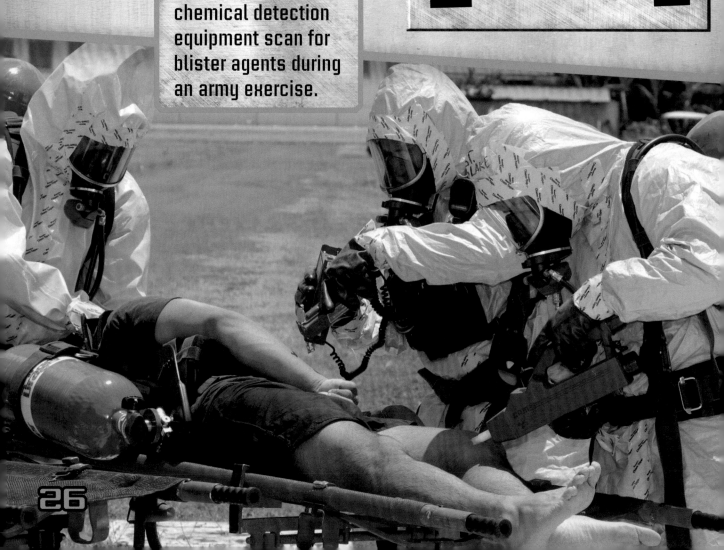

Lewisite, like all chemical agents, is extremely dangerous. A person who has had contact with lewisite must be treated quickly. Any clothing that has liquid lewisite on it must be removed. Clothing should not be pulled over the head, but should be cut off instead. This lessens the risk of the chemical touching the skin, eyes, or mouth.

Because lewisite contains arsenic, it has some effects that are similar to arsenic poisoning.

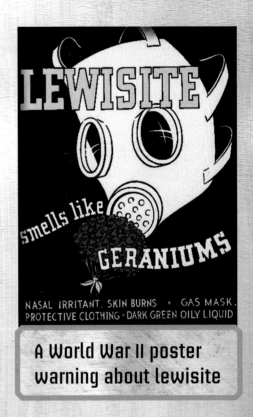

A World War II poster warning about lewisite

LEWISITE FACT FILE:

TYPE: Blister agent

APPEARANCE: Colorless liquid that can have a flowerlike smell

STRENGTH: Lewisite can get through cloth, and even rubber clothing

SYMPTOMS: Fluid-filled blisters, pain, and itching on the skin. If breathed in it causes pain and vomiting. It can also cause low blood pressure, known as "lewisite shock."

TREATMENT: Washing off the poison as soon as possible. There is an antidote, known as British anti-lewisite.

PROTECTING AGAINST AGENTS

There are several ways to protect yourself from a chemical attack. The lowest level of protection is to wear a gas mask. The types of protective clothing needed depend on the type of threat. The highest level of protection is a complete chemical-resistant suit with its own air supply.

The soldiers below are wearing high-level protection for an exercise. Here, they are sponging chemical agents off their suits, after a **simulated** chemical attack.

Air Force specialists demonstrate how to decontaminate each other after a chemical attack.

Researchers at Oregon State University have recently discovered compounds that can destroy chemical agents such as sarin gas. These new compounds may be able to be made into a clothlike material and used to make protective clothing. It would act kind of like a self-cleaning suit!

Protective suits used to be made of rubber, which was very hot and sweaty to wear. Nowadays, clothing is made with a layer of a substance called carbon, in between two layers of material. The carbon allows sweat to pass through. It also absorbs chemical agents and keeps them from touching the skin.

Shelters can be made to protect groups of people, too, and to supply air filtered by carbon.

GLOSSARY

algae: Plantlike living things, without roots or stems, that live in water.

anesthetic: Medicine to make feeling or pain go away.

antidote: A remedy to counteract the effects of poison.

binary chemical weapons: Chemical weapons in which the toxic agent in its active state is not contained within the weapon.

chemicals: Matter that can be mixed with other matter to cause changes.

chlorine: A greenish-yellow gas.

contaminates: Makes something unusable by adding poisons to it.

defoliant: A chemical that removes the leaves from trees and plants.

FBI: The Federal Bureau of Investigation.

fiction: Something told or written that is not fact.

hazmat: Hazardous materials.

hostage: A person held captive as a pledge that promises will be kept or terms met by another.

incapacitating: Making something incapable.

incinerated: Burned to ashes.

nerve agent: A dangerous chemical agent that interferes with nerve impulses.

neutralized: Made ineffective.

nonlethal: Not deadly.

religious cult: A small religious group regarded as extreme or dangerous.

sarin: A nerve gas.

simulated: Pretended.

tabun: A nerve gas.

toxins: Poisons made by a plant or an animal that harm another plant or animal.

weapon of mass destruction: A weapon that can kill or harm a large number of humans or cause great damage.

FOR MORE INFORMATION

BOOKS

Bearce, Stephanie. *Top Secret Files: The Cold War: Secrets, Special Missions, and Hidden Facts about the CIA, KGB, and MI6*. Austin, TX: Prufrock Press, 2015.

Fowler, Will. *The Story of Modern Weapons and Warfare* (A Journey Through History). New York, NY: Rosen, 2011.

Nardo, Don. *Invisible Weapons: The Science of Biological and Chemical Warfare* (Headline Science). North Mankato, MN: Compass Point Books, 2010.

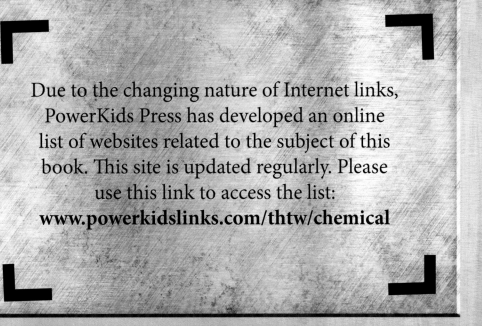

Due to the changing nature of Internet links, PowerKids Press has developed an online list of websites related to the subject of this book. This site is updated regularly. Please use this link to access the list: **www.powerkidslinks.com/thtw/chemical**

INDEX